Bobby

Through his appearances on television, and the story-telling sessions he has held in libraries, schools and at parties in Australia, New Zealand and South Africa as well as in almost every part of Britain, H. E. Todd can claim to be the best known story-teller in the world.

Here are nine stories about his favourite character, Bobby Brewster, the boy to whom the most extraordinary things happen.

BOBBY BREWSTER'S SQUITTEN
(OR KIRREL)
NAME. PEEPER (BECAUSE IT SAYS PEEP)
HEAD - SMALL
TAIL - HUGE
FUR - LONG AND GREY
SEX - FEMALE
AGE - 9 WEEKS - 2½ DAYS
FAVOURITE FOOD
SARDINES
HABITS

H. E. TODD

Bobby Brewster's scarecrow

Illustrated by Lilian Buchanan

KNIGHT BOOKS
Hodder & Stoughton

ISBN 0 340 16102 7

First published 1968 by Brockhampton Press Ltd
This edition first published 1972 by Knight Books,
the paperback division of Brockhampton Press Ltd (now
Hodder & Stoughton Children's Books) Leicester
Fourth impression 1976

Printed and bound in Great Britain
by Cox & Wyman Ltd, London, Reading and Fakenham

Contents

Introduction

He's still at it you see. Bobby Brewster is going about his ordinary everyday jobs and managing to find magic wherever he goes.

I would like to use a magic postbox myself, and I certainly wish I had been to a school where there was a magic master like Mr Limcano.

But this sort of thing only happens to Bobby Brewster, so the next best thing to do is to read about it.

I have had a lot of help with this book. When I told Bobby Brewster stories in libraries and schools I always asked for suggestions for more stories; and here are the names of the children who very kindly wrote to me, and whose ideas have been used in the stories in this book – Kevin Ashcroft, Kevin Bexley, Susan Bonner, Elspeth Connalty, Brenda Dover, Lorraine Elliott, Patricia Fleming, David Grant, Diane Hall, Jenny Hurst, Mary Husan, Daniel Isbister, Pauline Ling, Howard Lord, Rosemaria McCann, Melanie McClure, Neil Craig McKenzie, Lorna Messina, Tony Parsloe, Kim Pereira, Stephen Perrott, Stephanie Platt, Gordon Robson, Linda Stephens, Julie Summers, Diane Swaine, and Karen Whiteford.

H. E. TODD

The unscarecrow

Mr Brewster – that's Bobby Brewster's father – is not fond of gardening, so for one afternoon a week, on Tuesdays, the Brewsters have a gardener called Mr Petherick (Pethers for short). At the end of the garden Pethers has a vegetable patch with potatoes and beans and peas and cabbages and lettuces and things. Pethers is very proud of his vegetable garden, as well he might be, but he has a lot of trouble with the birds.

Now birds may be very cheeky and pretty

things to look at – indeed they are – but they seem to have nothing to do all day except fly about and eat. For most of them worms are their main course, which seems an odd choice to me but doesn't worry Pethers. After that they peck at the peas and other vegetables, and for pudding they finish up with a jolly good go at the strawberries and apples and other fruit. This really does annoy Pethers, so you can understand why he often calls the birds a 'dratted nuisance'.

Well, Pethers tried all sorts of ways for frightening the birds away. He put up red bottles on tops of poles and dangled strips of silver paper from string, but that wasn't any use. Then he bought two of those windmill things that whizz round and round, but the noise they made annoyed Mrs Brewster when she was working in the kitchen far more than it worried the birds.

In the end Pethers said, 'There's nothing for it. We shall have to make a scarecrow.'

Bobby Brewster thought that was a jolly good idea, not because of the birds, but because the idea of making a scarecrow appealed to him, so he offered to make it himself. He asked his mother to cut out and sew up the head and body from sacking. Then he filled it with straw. After that he had to dress it, and he got hold of some old torn trousers and a bright red pullover full of holes, and he bought a very old cap at a jumble sale for tuppence to save having to make any hair.

Well, that was all very well, but it still hadn't got a face. It was just a blank with a cap on top, which looked silly. Bobby can't paint very well, so he asked his father to paint one for him.

'What sort of a face do you want?' asked Mr Brewster.

'A ferocious face,' said Bobby. 'One to scare the birds away.'

His father painted a red nose to match the pullover, two cauliflower ears, two heavy black eyebrows, blue eyes, and a turned down mouth.

'There you are,' he said. 'That might even scare you away.'

'Thank you, Father,' said Bobby – but he wasn't so sure. The scarecrow had a ferocious face all right, but it looked to Bobby as if it was trying to be ferocious for fun, not because it was a really ferocious scarecrow. You know, the sort of face you make yourself when you are playing at lions and tigers but don't really mean it. In fact, in his heart of hearts Bobby thought it looked like a scarecrow he wouldn't mind talking to – if it could talk.

Never mind, Pethers was delighted with it. He tied it to two crossed poles with its arms stretched out, stuck the long pole in the vegetable patch, and thought his bird troubles were over.

How wrong he was. After it had been out for about a week Pethers said to Bobby, 'I can't think what's the matter with that silly scarecrow. I shall have to do away with it. It doesn't scare the birds away at all. It attracts them. Just look at it now.'

Bobby looked, and the scarecrow was simply covered with birds. There were two standing on its head, one on its nose, and lots and lots on its shoulders and arms. They were all twittering as if they were delighted to be there. What is more, from a distance it looked to Bobby Brewster as

if the scarecrow's mouth was turned up in a smile and it was just as delighted as the birds were.

'That's funny,' thought Bobby, and he walked towards the vegetable patch. By the time he reached there the birds had flown away and the scarecrow looked ferocious again – but still only funny ferocious and not serious ferocious.

Bobby turned his back and walked away a few steps. Then he suddenly turned round again. There was the scarecrow, with birds standing on its head, nose, shoulders and arms, and a silly grin on its face.

'Caught you!' said Bobby Brewster to himself.

At least, he thought he said it to himself, but he can't have done, because a very funny thing happened. The scarecrow answered him. It did, really.

'Caught me at what?' it asked.

'Caught you smiling at the birds,' said Bobby.

'And why not?' asked the scarecrow. 'They're cheeky little things. I like birds, don't you?'

'Yes, I suppose I do,' admitted Bobby. 'But you're different. You're a scarecrow and you're supposed to look ferocious and scare the birds away.'

'Lots of people are supposed to do things they don't do,' said the scarecrow. 'For instance, do you always take horrid medicine when your mother gives it to you?'

'Not always – if she isn't looking,' agreed Bobby.

'Very well then,' said the scarecrow, 'when you're not looking I don't scare the birds away. I smile at them because I like birds. Then they come and stand on my head, nose, shoulders and arms, and I tell them stories.'

This made Bobby Brewster feel rather worried.

'You know,' he said, 'this is all very well, but I'm afraid you won't be able to go on doing it much longer. Pethers – that's our gardener – thinks you're no good at your job. You're not a scarecrow at all. You're an unscarecrow. He says he's going to do away with you.'

This time the poor scarecrow made a different face altogether. Its mouth turned down at the corners and it started to cry. It was really a very upsetting sight.

'I don't want to be done away with,' it sobbed. 'I do no harm, and I'm perfectly happy out here with my friends the birds standing on my head, nose, shoulders and arms, listening to my stories. And they're happy too.'

'How do you know?' asked Bobby.

'Because they keep on telling me so,' said the scarecrow.

'Now *don't* tell me the birds can *talk*,' said Bobby Brewster.

'Certainly they can – to me,' said the scarecrow. 'Haven't you ever heard them twitter?'

'Yes, of course I have,' said Bobby. 'But that's not talking. It's just twittering.'

'You're quite wrong,' said the scarecrow. 'It's not twitter*ing*. It's twitter*talk*. And there's a great deal of difference. Baby birds do twitter*ing* and grown-up birds do twitter*talk*. If you promise to stand still and stay where you are, I will prove it to you.'

'I promise,' said Bobby.

'Good,' said the scarecrow. 'Now watch.' Then it called out – *'All right, birds, you can come and stand on me.'*

And they did. They had been hiding in the trees when they saw Bobby, but as soon as the scarecrow called to them they flew over and stood on its head, nose, shoulders and arms.

'Do you know,' said the scarecrow to the birds, 'Bobby Brewster says that Pethers the gardener

is going to do away with me, because instead of scaring you birds away, I smile at you and tell you stories. He says I'm not a scarecrow at all, but an unscarecrow.'

You never heard such a noise as those birds made. They hopped up and down and twittered and twittered – and if it is possible for birds to look furious, they really did look furious.

'What does all that mean?' asked Bobby.

'The birds say that if Pethers tries to do away with me they'll attack him and peck his eyes out,' said the scarecrow.

'Goodness me,' cried Bobby. 'We can't have

that. Pethers has enough trouble with his eyes already and has to wear glasses when he reads. Will you ask them why they keep on pecking at our vegetables and fruit?'

So the scarecrow did – and there was more twittering. At least it sounded like twitter*ing* to Bobby, but it must have been twitter*talk*, because after it had finished the scarecrow said, 'They say they *have* to eat something with worm, and ask how *you* would like just plain worm for your dinner without any vegetables and fruit.'

'I wouldn't like to eat worm at all, with or without vegetables and fruit,' said Bobby. 'Anyway, I wish they wouldn't eat *our* vegetables and fruit. That's what Pethers objects to, and I don't blame him.'

Then one little bird – the one on the scarecrow's nose – made a suggestion.

'It says,' explained the scarecrow, 'that if Pethers promises to leave me here and not do away with me, all the birds will only take worms from his garden and go next door for their vegetables and fruit.'

'Oh no,' said Bobby quickly, 'I'm afraid that won't do at all. Mr and Mrs Henderson who live next door are great friends of mine, and I *know* they like eating lots of vegetables and fruit, because I've been there to dinner and seen them.'

'Oh dear,' sighed the scarecrow. 'Whatever are we to do?'

Then Bobby Brewster had an idea.

'I'll tell you what,' he suggested. 'Supposing I bring the birds a nice dinner every day. I can bring lots of crumbs as well, not only bread crumbs but cake crumbs as well, and left overs from our own dinner. And once a week, for a special treat, I will bring sardine sandwiches.'

'That seems a jolly good idea to me,' said the scarecrow. 'I'll ask the birds what they think about it.'

So he did. And they agreed with a great deal of twitter*talk* that it would suit them very well. But they said there was no need for Mrs Brewster to trouble to make sardine sandwiches. They would be quite happy if Bobby brought out one plate with the sardines and another with bits of bread, and then they would peck at each plate in turn.

That is exactly what happens, and it always works very well indeed. The birds thoroughly enjoy the food that Bobby brings, and the unscarecrow sees that they behave themselves and don't peck at the vegetables and fruit in Pethers' garden. And that's not all. There is no question of the crows and starlings being greedy and finishing everything off before the smaller birds can get at it. They have their dinners one after the other without any quarrelling, and their table manners are perfect. So everyone, including Pethers, is perfectly happy.

Jump out and bite

How tidy is your bedroom? I'm afraid I can't give Bobby Brewster full marks for his. Mind you, I'm not one to blame him, because sometimes I can't give myself full marks for *my* bedroom either.

Not that I like bedrooms to be too tidy, or any other room for that matter. There are some houses where the sitting-room is so straight that you hardly dare sit on the sofa for fear of ruffling the cushions, and you talk in a hushed whisper in case your breath clouds the mirror on the wall. It doesn't seem like a home at all – more like a museum. On a visit you never stay long if you can help it and you are jolly glad to get away again.

However, there *is* a happy medium, and there are occasions when Bobby Brewster's bedroom is too untidy even for me, and certainly his mother. When he has left for school she goes upstairs to make his bed and finds the bedclothes all over the floor. One slipper is under the bed, and another covered by his old jeans slung on the chair. The school tie which he should have been wearing is all mixed up inside the bed-clothes, and the book he needed for that day's lessons has fallen behind the bedside table and is lying on the floor on its edge.

After a morning like that Mrs Brewster tries to be strict and tells Bobby when he comes home that he is not to do *anything* until he has tidied his room. Then he goes upstairs and crams everything that is lying about away in his chest of drawers. Not that *that* helps much except to make the place look tidy for a short time. When he next needs something in a hurry before going to school he has forgotten which drawer he put it in, so everything is turned out in a wild rush to find it and then the whole business starts all over again.

So this is the sort of conversation that takes place in the Brewster house day after day. And not only between Mrs Brewster and Bobby. Sometimes Mr Brewster is the culprit – but we won't go into that now.

Bobby Brewster (from upstairs): 'Mother, where are my clean stockings?'

Mrs Brewster (in the kitchen cooking breakfast): 'In your top long drawer where they always are, dear.'

Bobby Brewster: '*I* can't find them.'

Mrs Brewster: 'You haven't looked properly.'

Bobby Brewster: 'I have.'

Mrs Brewster: 'Then look again.'

Bobby Brewster (after a pause): 'I've found *one* stocking, but the other isn't there.'

Mrs Brewster: 'It *must* be.'

Bobby Brewster: 'Well, *I* can't find it.'

Mrs Brewster: 'Oh dear, I suppose I shall have to come and look myself.'

So she does – and the first thing she finds is the missing stocking, right on top of the clothes in the drawer. Then she always makes the same remark:

'Really, Bobby, did you expect it to jump out and bite you?' to which Bobby always replies, rather lamely, 'Well, *I* couldn't see it.'

Anyway, one morning during last November a very funny thing happened. It was rather cold, and Bobby Brewster decided that for the first time that winter he would wear gloves to school. He looked quickly inside the drawer where he thought they were kept, but they weren't on top, so he straight away shouted downstairs:

'Mother, where are my woollen gloves?'

'In the top right-hand drawer of your chest, dear.'

'Well, *I* can't find them.'

'Then look again.'

'I have looked – *oh*!'

'What's the matter, dear?'

'I've hurt my finger.'

Bobby came running downstairs, carrying his gloves in one hand, and shaking the other hand violently.

'What have you done to your hand?' asked his mother.

'I really don't know,' said Bobby. 'Just before I found my gloves I had a sudden pain in my little finger. Look at it.'

So Mrs Brewster did, and Bobby's little finger was all red.

'Never mind,' said Mrs Brewster. 'We'll put some witch hazel on it, and it will soon be better.'

So she did. And it was.

'I'm glad you found your gloves, anyway,' said Mrs Brewster. 'I knew you would if you looked properly. Did you expect them to jump out and bite you?'

Bobby didn't say anything, but it made him think.

The next day was football day at school. Bobby had got very muddy in his last game and he needed some clean football stockings, but when he opened the drawer where they were kept he couldn't find them.

'Mother, where are my clean football stockings?'

'In the top long drawer of your chest of drawers, dear.'

'Well – *I* can't find – *oh!*'

'What's the matter, dear?'

'I've hurt my toe.'

Bobby hobbled downstairs, carrying his football stockings.

'What have you done to your leg?' asked his mother.

'I don't really know,' said Bobby. 'Just before I found my football stockings I had a sudden pain in my big toe. Look at it.'

So Mrs Brewster did, and Bobby's big toe was all red.

'Never mind,' said Mrs Brewster. 'We'll put some witch hazel on it and it will soon be better.'

So she did. And it was.

'I'm glad you found your football stockings,

anyway,' said Mrs Brewster. 'I knew you would if you looked properly. Did you expect them to jump out and bite you?'

Bobby didn't say anything, but he thought even harder, because his big toe *did* feel rather as if it had been bitten..

The next day was clean vest day. Sometimes Mrs Brewster puts Bobby's clean vest out ready for the morning, but she had been late to bed the night before, so she had forgotten. When she heard Bobby jump out of bed she called up the stairs:

'Bobby, don't forget to put a clean vest on.'

'All right, Mother,' he replied. But when he opened the drawer he couldn't find one, so he shouted –

'Mother, where *is* my clean vest?'

'In the bottom long drawer of your chest of drawers, dear.'

'Well, *I* can't – *oh!*'

'What's the matter, dear?'

'I've hurt my chest.'

Bobby ran downstairs in his pants, carrying his vest.

'What have you done to your chest, dear?' asked his mother.

'I don't really know,' said Bobby. 'Just before I found my vest I had a sudden sting. Look at it.'

So Mrs Brewster looked – and there was a bright red spot on Bobby's chest.

'It looks just like a bite,' said Mrs Brewster. 'Never mind. We'll put some witch hazel on it and it will soon be better.'

So she did. And it was.

'I'm glad you found your vest, anyway,' she said. 'Did you expect it to jump out and bite you?'

Bobby didn't say anything, but he wondered. *Had* his vest jumped out and bitten him?

The next day was clean pants day, and for once Bobby remembered when he got out of bed. He went and opened the bottom long drawer of his chest of drawers, and at first he couldn't find any clean pants. Then he started to shout –

'Mother, where are my . . . ?'

He suddenly stopped. No. Before asking any more he would look again, more carefully. So he did. Yes – his pants *were* there in the drawer after all, under his shirts. He started to put them on.

His mother called from downstairs, 'What is it you want, dear?'

'Nothing, Mother,' answered Bobby. 'I wanted some clean pants, but I've found them now.'

'Good boy,' said his mother. 'At last you've found something for yourself.'

I think Bobby was not only a good boy, but a

very sensible boy, don't you? After all, it's bad enough to be bitten by your gloves in the little finger, your football stockings in the big toe and your vest in the chest, isn't it? But when it comes to being bitten by a pair of pants, it might be a far more painful thing. Just in time, Bobby had thought so, anyway, so he wasn't taking any chances.

And I don't blame him, do you?

And from that day to this he hasn't taken any chances when looking for any of his clothes, so Mrs Brewster has never needed to ask, 'Did you expect them to jump out and bite you?'

Which is a very good thing, isn't it?

Letters by return

When the new Post Office was built near his home, Bobby Brewster said at once that the postbox in the front wall looked magic to him. If people asked him why, he couldn't explain, but just said that it had a magic look about it. Of course everyone laughed, but by the time you have finished reading this story I'm sure you will have to agree with Bobby Brewster.

The first funny thing that happened was when he posted a parcel for his father. Perhaps I ought to explain that the postbox in the front wall of the Post Office is the sort with a wide mouth where you can post parcels or even put your arm inside if you are feeling silly enough. And when you do post a parcel there is a loud 'plonk' when it lands on the floor.

At least, there is *usually* a 'plonk', but when Bobby Brewster posted that particular parcel, instead of the 'plonk', a voice inside shouted, 'Oh!' It did, really. Of course Bobby was very surprised, but when he said afterwards that it must be a magic postbox his father explained that there was nothing magic about it, but the voice was a postman in the sorting office shouting 'Oh!' when the parcel landed on his head.

Secretly Bobby was rather disappointed about that, because he was excited at the idea of a magic postbox. Then another funny thing happened. The very next day he went to post a letter and as he was feeling in a silly mood he put his arm inside the letter box, right up to the elbow, before letting go of the letter. Then, much to his surprise, someone shook his hand. And that wasn't all. After that, when he placed his mouth close to the opening and shouted, 'Good luck,' a voice shouted back, 'And the same to you.'

Of course that made him think that the postbox really was magic, but again his father said no, it must be a very jolly postman in the sorting office who shook his hand and shouted back to him just for fun.

Bobby didn't want to argue with his father, but he wasn't so sure. He still felt that there was something magic-*looking* about that postbox, and he decided to go on using it whenever he had something to post, just in case.

Bobby has a very nice cousin called Barbara who lives in Northern Ireland. Well, her birthday came soon after that and he bought her a smart red purse for a birthday present. He packed it neatly in a large envelope and went to the Post Office to buy some stamps. Then he stuck the stamps on the envelope, carried it to the postbox in the front wall, put his arm right inside, and let go. There was a 'plonk' when it fell on the floor, and that was that. Nothing funny happened – at least Bobby didn't think so at that time. But when he got home he soon changed his mind.

Lying on the doormat was a letter addressed to Master Robert Brewster. He opened it, feeling rather pleased because he doesn't often receive letters, and this is what it said:

Dear Bobby,

Thank you very much for the lovely red purse. It was just what I wanted.

Love from
Barbara

This time surely it must have been the magic postbox. Otherwise how could Bobby possibly post a parcel to Northern Ireland and run straight home to find a letter thanking him for it? But, do you know, even then his father didn't agree. He was away on business at the time, and when Bobby told him about it on his return, he said it couldn't have happened just like that and that Bobby must have got his dates muddled up. 'After all,' he said, 'whoever heard of a magic postbox?' And you can hardly blame him, can you?

But a few days later something happened that convinced even Mr Brewster. It was during the Christmas holidays, and Cousin Barbara was coming from Northern Ireland to stay with the Brewsters for a week. Bobby was very excited, because his mother and father had promised to let him have a party and invite all his friends to meet her, so he decided to write and tell Barbara about the party and at the same time to buy some invitation cards to send to his friends. When he posted the letter to Barbara the funniest thing of all happened. In his usual silly way

Bobby put his arm inside before letting go of the letter. No one said 'Oh!' or shook hands with him, but to his great surprise he felt someone put a packet into his hand, and when he took it out he found he was holding a bundle of letters tied round with a ribbon. He looked at them, and they were all addressed to Master Robert Brewster.

Well, he couldn't run home fast enough, and

I'm not surprised, are you? When he opened the first letter it was from Cousin Barbara.

It said:

Dear Bobby,

Thank you for your letter. I am looking forward very much to next week, and please tell Auntie and Uncle that I think it is very kind of them to arrange a special party while I am staying with you.

Love from
Barbara

That was surprising enough, wasn't it? Once again Bobby had received a reply to a letter at the same time as sending it. But wait till you hear what was in the other letters. All of them were from his friends saying they would be delighted to come to his party the following week. They were, really!

How on earth did they *know* about his party? In his pocket was a new packet of invitation cards which Bobby had only bought that morning, and he hadn't even written on them, let alone posted them to his friends. Yet here in his hand were letters from all the same friends thanking him for inviting them!

Well, that really *did* prove it, didn't it? Even Mr Brewster had to admit that the postbox in the front wall of the Post Office must be magic.

But only for Bobby Brewster himself. It's not the slightest use hoping to get a quick answer by asking Bobby to write your letters and post them for you. It doesn't work. I know, because I've tried several times. It merely annoys the magic postbox so that the replies take weeks and weeks to arrive, or sometimes are even lost in the post.

The Thingamybob

A dear old lady lives near Bobby Brewster's home and her name is Mrs Fittleworth. She lives by herself in a large house and she has rather straggly white hair and always wears exactly the same clothes whatever the time of year. She attends the same church as the Brewsters do and she always goes to everything. No church concert ever takes place without Mrs Fittleworth buying one of the front seat tickets. She turns up to every bazaar and buys lots of oddments that could never be any use to her. She has been turning up for years and years, always looking exactly the same, and always smiling graciously.

Everybody knows Mrs Fittleworth and everybody likes her too, because she is so kind. She has a habit of asking people to tea. They arrive at half past four and leave at exactly six o'clock. Bobby Brewster has been with his mother three times, and although he thinks it is very kind of Mrs Fittleworth to invite him, he hopes she doesn't do it too often because she always gives him the same book to read and it isn't very interesting.

There is one jolly good thing about the teas though – there are always plenty of sardine sandwiches. As you know, Bobby is very fond of sardine sandwiches and he never feels rude when he eats at least six at tea with Mrs Fittleworth. That is because Mrs Fittleworth seems to like sardine sandwiches just as much as Bobby Brewster. The last time she ate ten of them. She did, really! Bobby Brewster was just as surprised as you probably are, but he knows it is true because he counted them.

Mrs Fittleworth has one drawback. Well, perhaps it isn't quite fair to call it a drawback, because no harm is done and in fact everyone treats it as rather a joke. She is very absent-minded and she can never remember names. If there is a concert at the Town Hall you can be sure that Mrs Fittleworth will arrive late, looking flustered, having first been to the Church Hall by mistake. The last three times she has met Bobby Brewster in the street she has smiled kindly and said, 'Hello Richard', 'Hello Henry' and 'Hello John', and when Mrs Brewster arrived for tea the other day she was rather surprised to be asked, 'And how is dear Mr Fletcher?' Actually that was rather a difficult question to answer, because Mr Fletcher has been dead for three years, but Mrs Brewster didn't want to alarm Mrs Fittleworth, so she just said, 'Very well, thank you, and he sends you his best wishes.'

After tea on that occasion, while Bobby was trying to look interested in the book he was reading for the third time, the ladies were talking and Mrs Brewster happened to mention that it was Bobby's birthday the next Tuesday.

'Fancy that,' said Mrs Fittleworth. 'How time does fly!' and she smiled at Bobby. Of course, Bobby smiled back, but he didn't think any more about it until, the next Tuesday morning, a rather unexpected thing happened. Bobby had finished his breakfast – his birthday breakfast – and he was sitting by the window looking at a book that had been given to him, when he saw Mrs Fittleworth coming up the garden path carrying a parcel. His mother was upstairs at the time, so he went to open the front door.

'Good morning, Mrs Fittleworth,' he said. 'Won't you come in?'

'No thank you, dear,' said Mrs Fittleworth. 'I just thought I would bring you a little present. Many happy returns of the day, William.'

Bobby knew she must mean him, so he took the parcel and said, 'Thank you very much, Mrs Fittleworth,' and she went away.

Before opening his parcel Bobby looked at the writing on the outside. It said, 'Many happy returns of the day to dear Charles.' At first Bobby nearly called Mrs Fittleworth back, but then he remembered the mistake she always made, so he changed his mind. It was quite a large parcel and Bobby felt rather excited as he opened it. After all, Mrs Fittleworth had never given him a present before and even if it was addressed to 'Charles', it was still a pleasant surprise.

When the parcel was opened it was difficult to say whether it was a pleasant surprise or not, because Bobby couldn't make out what the present was meant to be. It was mostly made of wood, and looked like a sort of a frame. There was a little wheel, and a sort of a handle, with some string which seemed like a sort of a pulley. In fact, altogether it was just a sort of a present.

At that moment Bobby heard his mother coming downstairs.

'Mother,' he said. 'Mrs Fittleworth has just brought me a birthday present.'

'How very kind of her,' said Mrs Brewster. 'What is it?'

'I don't know,' said Bobby Brewster. 'Come and look.'

Mrs Brewster came into the sitting-room and saw what was on the table. 'Why,' she said. 'It's the Thingamybob,' and she started to laugh.

'Whatever do you mean?' asked Bobby Brewster.

'Well,' explained Mrs Brewster, 'for the last five years this Thingamybob has been on sale at the Church Bazaar. Someone always buys it and then the next year it is given back to be sold again. The funny thing is that it is always given back to be sold at a different stall. It has been on the woodwork stall, the white elephant stall and the handicraft stall. Last year someone thought it was a knitting machine so it was on the knitting stall, and at the sale last Saturday it appeared again on the toy stall.'

'So I suppose Mrs Fittleworth thought it was a toy, and when she heard it was my birthday she gave it to me,' said Bobby.

'Yes,' said Mrs Brewster. 'Wasn't that kind of her?'

'Um, yes,' said Bobby Brewster, but he didn't sound very grateful.

Well, of course, the next day was time for Bobby to write his 'thank yous'. He is getting on well with his writing at school and he wrote some very neat and well composed letters. He thought he had finished, but then Mrs Brewster said, 'What about Mrs Fittleworth?'

'Oh dear!' said Bobby. 'I had forgotten about her.'

When he started writing Mrs Fittleworth her letter he found it more difficult. 'Dear Mrs Fittleworth, Thank you very much for the lovely thingamybob you gave me' didn't sound quite right, and it was no better to put, 'I have had a fine time playing with that thingamybob you you gave me yesterday morning.' Besides, it was not true. Bobby wondered if it would be good manners to ask, 'Dear Mrs Fittleworth, Thank you for the birthday present, but what is it?' and his mother said, 'No, it wouldn't.' In the end he just wrote, 'Dear Mrs Fittleworth, It was very kind of you to give me a birthday present,' and left it at that.

For the next few weeks, although he likes Mrs Fittleworth, Bobby tried to avoid meeting her in case she asked him any questions about the Thingamybob. One afternoon she called at the Brewsters', and Bobby was very careful to keep

it up in his bedroom out of sight. He had a shock though when she suddenly said, 'Tell me, Christopher,' because he wondered what was coming next. But luckily she only went on to ask, 'How are you getting on at school?' So that was all right.

Well, time passed and no more questions were asked, so Bobby Brewster began to feel that Mrs Fittleworth must have forgotten all about it. He was quite right, as you will see from the end of this story.

The next spring Mrs Fittleworth was ill and had to stay in bed. Bobby went with his mother to visit her, and she seemed very touched because he took her a bunch of daffodils.

The following week there was a church jumble sale and as Mrs Brewster was rather tired of dusting the Thingamybob when she tidied his bedroom, she asked Bobby if it could go for jumble. 'After all,' she said, 'Mrs Fittleworth is ill and won't be able to go to the sale, and in any case I am sure she has forgotten all about it' – so Bobby agreed.

Imagine how they felt the next Saturday when

they went to the jumble sale in the afternoon and there was Mrs Fittleworth. Of course they were delighted to see she was better, but they watched anxiously as she looked at the stalls. To their horror she picked up the Thingamybob.

They need not have worried though. On her way out Mrs Fittleworth caught sight of Mrs Brewster and Bobby and she made her way over to them.

'I didn't expect to see you here, Mrs Fittleworth,' said Mrs Brewster. 'Are you feeling better?'

'Yes,' said Mrs Fittleworth. 'I am much better and do you know why?'

'No,' said Mrs Brewster.

'Because my friends were all so kind to me while I was ill in bed.'

Then she turned to Bobby and smiled.

'Do you know,' she said. 'Whenever I looked at the lovely daffodils by my bedside I thought of dear Richard who had given them to me, and so I made up my mind to get better quickly and buy him something at the jumble sale. Here you are, Richard.'

Can you guess what Mrs Fittleworth handed to Bobby? I am sure you can.

It was the Thingamybob again!

The washing-machine

Does your mother use a washing-machine at home? Mrs Brewster used an old one for a long time, but it sploshed water all over the kitchen floor. It was probably partly her own fault, but anyway she got jolly fed up with it, and suggested to Mr Brewster that they bought a new one. He didn't say 'Yes' at once, because new washing-machines are rather expensive, but she went on suggesting it until he agreed.

A smart affair it was, too; all white and gleaming. It was one of the new automatic kind that does everything except fold up the washing and put it in the airing cupboard. Mrs Brewster was very proud of it.

Bobby Brewster liked it, too. It had a glass porthole in front and he could watch the clothes inside whizzing round and round. When they were whizzing fast all the blue, green, and white shirts and pyjamas and things were mixed up and made a pretty pattern in the porthole. When the machine stopped the clothes were mixed up so much that it took quite a time to unravel the sleeves and pyjama cords, but it was worth it to see how clean everything was.

Then, one morning during the holidays, Bobby was in the kitchen watching his mother using the washing-machine, when the telephone rang.

Does your mother ever talk for hours and hours on the telephone? Mrs Brewster does, especially when she is talking to her cousin, Mrs Patricia Rogers, and that is who had rung her up that morning. There must have been something even more interesting than usual to talk about, because the conversation went on and on, while Bobby waited in the kitchen.

Then a very funny thing happened. A voice inside the washing-machine cried, 'Help!' It did, really. Bobby couldn't believe his ears until it shouted again, '*Help! Help!*'

He didn't know what to do. He didn't want to interrupt his mother, and yet he had been told never to fiddle with the washing-machine when it was going. He had nearly decided to switch it off when, luckily, it stopped by itself.

Bobby anxiously opened the front. He half expected to see a little man inside, or something extraordinary like that. After all, who else could have shouted 'Help!'? But there was nothing there except a solid bunch of mixed-up clothes, and he tipped them into the basket.

When his mother returned to the kitchen she saw him trying to unravel the clothes, and she looked anxiously at his hands. If they had been in their usual state they wouldn't have done much good to clothes that had just been washed; but for once they were perfectly clean, so she didn't say anything except, 'Thank you for helping me.' Bobby didn't say anything either. He thought that if he told his mother that he was helping because something inside the washing-machine had shouted 'Help!' it might sound silly. I think he was quite right about that, don't you?

Anyway, all the clothes were sorted. Some were ironed and others folded and put in the airing cupboard. Bobby Brewster had almost forgotten about the voice shouting 'Help!', when another funny thing happened.

It was just before his winter term started at

school, and he thought he would practise football in the garden. His mother gave him his clean football sweater to wear because it was rather chilly. As soon as he took it outside and put it on he felt rather giddy, and when he ran to kick his football he missed it completely and fell sideways. Then when he got up, everything was going round and round and he fell sideways again.

'Whatever's the matter?' he said to himself.

At least, he thought he said it to himself, but he can't have done because a voice answered him. It did, really.

It said – 'I'm the matter.'

'Who are you?' asked Bobby.

'I'm your football sweater,' said the voice.

'Whoever heard a football sweater talking?' asked Bobby.

'You did,' said the voice. 'In fact you once even heard a football sweater shouting.'

'When?' asked Bobby Brewster.

'When I shouted "Help!" inside the washing-machine the other day,' said the voice.

'Goodness gracious, was that you?' asked Bobby, very surprised.

'It certainly was,' said the football sweater. 'And I should jolly well think so, too. Putting me in a washing-machine with all the white linens indeed.'

'Why not?' asked Bobby. 'It must be jolly good fun, like going round in a very fast roundabout.'

'That's all very well,' said the football sweater. 'But some people feel sick if they're on a roundabout for too long. And they'd feel sicker still if they were covered in soapsuds and then soaked in very hot water as well.'

'I hadn't thought of that,' said Bobby. 'But,

after all, Mother only wanted to make you clean. And see how lovely you look now. Whiter than white.'

'That's more by luck than judgement,' said the football sweater. 'I think your mother must have been so excited about her new washing-machine that she forgot to read the instructions. Don't you realize that I'm made of wool? I shouldn't be washed with very hot water for four minutes. I'm far too fragile and precious. I should only be rinsed in tepid water for half a minute. No wonder I was giddy when you put me on.'

'Oh dear,' said Bobby, 'I'm very sorry. Mother is so busy that she couldn't have had time to read the instructions properly. I shall have to tell her about it.'

'You jolly well will,' said the football sweater. 'And you can tell her from me that she's lucky that I only got giddy this time. If she makes the same mistake again it will be far more serious. I shall shrink so much that when you put me on you will look like a skinned rabbit.'

'Thanks for the warning,' said Bobby Brewster. 'I should hate to look like a skinned rabbit.'

Well, he *did* warn his mother in a roundabout way. He didn't actually say anything about his football sweater shouting 'Help!' inside the washing-machine when it felt giddy. He thought it might sound silly. But when his mother was sorting out the dirty clothes next time, he helped her and was very careful to put his football sweater with the woollen things.

'There you are, Mother,' he said. 'You see I've put all the woollens together.'

'Thank you very much for your help,' said his mother. 'You've done it perfectly.' And she wondered how on earth Bobby knew how to sort out clothes for a washing-machine. But I know. And so do you, don't you?

And since then, another funny thing has happened. Not only is Bobby playing far better football, but while he's playing it he always seems to look quite clean in his football sweater. Which is a thing that never happened before.

The squitten

Mr Limcano cannot really be described as ordinary. He wears rather funny clothes, with bow ties and coloured waistcoats and things like that. But the boys of Miss Trenham's school don't make fun of him because of it. Oh dear me, no. They all like him too much for that, and not just because he is a magician. Do you know the real reason? Mr Limcano likes boys himself, and they realize it, so it is hardly surprising that they like him back, is it?

One day in class they were having nature study. Of course they usually talk about trees and plants and butterflies and tadpoles and things like that, but this time Mr Limcano suddenly asked:

'Have any of you boys got a pet animal at home?'

Well, you never heard such a noise. Nearly *all* the boys had a dog or a cat or a rabbit or some goldfish or a budgerigar, and they all wanted to talk about them at once.

'One at a time please,' said Mr Limcano, and he asked each boy in turn to describe the habits of his own particular pet so that they could compare them. Then he got to Bobby Brewster.

Now Bobby has a cat called Tawny and a dog called Tipsy at home. But not long ago the Brewsters were given another kitten. At least, it is a *sort* of a kitten, and you will know what I mean when I go on with this story.

'Please sir,' said Bobby Brewster, 'I've just been given a new pet. A sort of a kitten.'

'What do you mean by a sort of a kitten?' asked Mr Limcano.

'Well sir,' said Bobby, 'I suppose it *is* a kitten really, but it doesn't exactly look like one.'

'What *does* it look like?' asked Mr Limcano.

'It's got lots of long grey fur, rather a small head, very small ears, and a long bushy tail,' said Bobby.

'It sounds more like a squirrel to me,' said Mr Limcano.

'It *looks* rather like a squirrel,' agreed Bobby,

'but I know it must be a kitten really, because I've seen its brother, and he's a ginger kitten for certain.'

'That's very interesting,' said Mr Limcano. 'A kitten that looks more like a squirrel. Perhaps it ought to be called a squitten.'

'Perhaps so,' said Bobby. 'Or a kirrel,' and the boys laughed.

'I really think we must hear more about this remarkable animal,' said Mr Limcano. 'So we'll start by drawing it on the blackboard. From your description it must look rather like this.'

Now Mr Limcano draws very well, and sometimes his drawings are very funny – that is another reason why the boys like him so much. Considering the fact that he had only heard Bobby describe his squitten but had never seen it, his drawing was quite remarkable. It made the boys laugh, too. They had never seen anything like it. But Bobby Brewster had.

'Yes sir,' he cried. 'That's exactly like Peeper.'

'Like who?' asked Mr Limcano.

'Peeper,' said Bobby. 'We call it Peeper because instead of saying "Miaow" it says "Peep".'

'More and more remarkable,' said Mr Limcano. 'We must record all these facts on the board.'

So he wrote above the drawing:

Bobby Brewster's Squitten (or Kirrel)

And then:

Name: Peeper (because it says 'peep')
Head: Small
Tail: Huge
Fur: Long and grey

Then he asked, 'Is it a girl or a boy squitten?'

'A girl,' said Bobby. 'At least, I *think* so, but I'm not quite sure.'

'Very well, we'll give you the benefit of the doubt,' said Mr Limcano, and he wrote:

Sex: Female

And then asked, 'How old?'

'Nine weeks and two and a half days,' said Bobby, so that went up on the board as well:

Age: 9 weeks $2\frac{1}{2}$ days

'What does it eat?' asked Mr Limcano.

'Almost anything that's left lying about,' said Bobby, 'but mostly cat food and fish.'

'What is its *favourite* food?'

'Sardines,' said Bobby without hesitation, and Mr Limcano wrote:

Favourite food: Sardines

'So far so good,' said Mr Limcano. 'Now, about its habits. What are they?'

'Ridiculous,' said Bobby.

'What do you mean by that?' asked Mr Limcano.

'Well, it rushes up and down curtains and along the piano keys, and crawls inside paper bags, and chases flies and balls of wool, and jumps on everything and knocks things down. And all for no particular reason.'

'That must be very fatiguing,' said Mr Limcano. 'Doesn't it ever sleep?'

'Yes,' said Bobby. 'But even then it's ridiculous. It doesn't lie *on* things, it nearly lies *off* them.'

'I don't see how that's possible,' said Mr Limcano.

'Well, when it's lying on a chair, three of its legs and its tail are hanging over the edge,' explained Bobby.

'However does it keep up?' asked Mr Limcano.

'It doesn't always,' said Bobby. 'Sometimes it falls down in the middle of its sleep, but that doesn't make any difference. It jumps up and lies in exactly the same silly position again.'

'I see what you mean when you say its habits are ridiculous,' said Mr Limcano. 'We'll have to put that up too I'm afraid.' So he wrote:

Habits: Ridiculous

By then it was dinner time, and Bobby left the classroom feeling rather proud that everything about his new pet Peeper, including its picture, was up on Mr Limcano's blackboard.

Now that day he was having dinner at school. And a jolly good dinner it was, too. They started with mince and potatoes, and Bobby enjoyed it so much that he went up for a second helping.

'I put an extra plateful out by mistake, Bobby,' said Miss Trenham, who was serving the dinner, 'so you can have that instead of a second helping. It's on the table behind me.'

But it wasn't. The plate was there all right, but the mince had disappeared.

'Where has it gone?' said Miss Trenham. 'I know I put it there.'

'I think that kitten ate it, Miss Trenham,' said Miss Horton, who was helping her.

'What kitten?' asked Miss Trenham, 'I don't allow kittens in here.'

'Well, I've just seen one,' said Miss Horton. 'And a funny-looking animal it was. Just like a squirrel.'

That made Bobby think, but he took a second

helping of mince, and then tucked in to the trifle. As he was finishing he heard Miss Trenham shout, 'SHOO – you silly animal. Get out of here.' And he looked up just in time to see a kitten streak out of the door. What is more, as far as Bobby could tell from the streak, the kitten looked like a squitten – in fact it looked just like Peeper.

'It *can't* be Peeper,' thought Bobby.

But there were more surprising things to come. When Bobby went back to his classroom after dinner break he was walking with Mr Limcano, and as they were passing Miss Horton's classroom she came running to the door.

'There was a ridiculous animal in my classroom when I came in,' she cried, 'running up and down the curtains. Now it's disappeared.'

'What did it look like?' asked Mr Limcano.

'Like a mixture between a kitten and a squirrel,' said Miss Horton. 'I've never seen anything like it before.'

Mr Limcano turned to Bobby. 'It sounds to me like Peeper,' he said.

'It *can't* be,' said Bobby Brewster. 'Peeper lives at my home which is a mile away.'

'Well, it's very extraordinary,' said Mr Limcano.

But he didn't realize quite how extraordinary it really was. When they went into their own classroom the boys who were already there cried,

'Please, sir, someone's rubbed out that lovely picture of the squitten you drew on your black-board.'

'What a silly thing to do,' said Mr Limcano. But, do you know, when he inquired, all of the boys protested that *they* certainly hadn't done it.

'We wouldn't *think* of doing such a thing, sir,' they said. 'We *liked* your picture.'

Just as the inquiries finished there was a loud crash in Miss Horton's next-door classroom. Mr Limcano ran in to see what was the matter, and Miss Horton cried, 'It's that ridiculous animal again. It jumped in my cupboard and knocked all the books down. There it is. Look!'

Mr Limcano took one look and immediately ran back to his own classroom.

'Bobby,' he said. 'It *is* Peeper.'

'It *can't* be, sir,' said Bobby. 'I'm sure it can't. Why don't you ring up my mother and ask if Peeper is at home? That will prove it.'

So Mr Limcano did. He went to Miss Trenham's office and rang the Brewster house, and Mrs Brewster told him that Peeper was lying fast asleep on the sofa in her sitting-room.

'At least,' she added, 'she isn't exactly lying *on* the sofa. She's three-quarters *off* it. But she's fast asleep all the same. I don't know how she does it.'

When Mr Limcano went back to his class and told the boys what Mrs Brewster had said, Bobby Brewster had an idea.

'Do you know, sir,' he said. 'I think you must have drawn a *magic* picture of Peeper without knowing it. You know how magic you *can* be. Your picture of the squitten must have jumped off the blackboard and is running about the school.'

'Oh dear,' said Mr Limcano, 'this is not the first time my magic has got out of hand. We can't have a picture of a ridiculous animal like that let loose. It might create chaos.'

'It will, sir,' said Bobby Brewster. 'The real Peeper often creates chaos at home.'

Then he had another idea.

'Sir,' he suggested, 'why don't you draw a picture of some sardines on the board. Then the picture of the squitten might come back and eat the picture of the sardines and you can rub them both out so there won't be any more trouble.'

'That's a very good idea,' said Mr Limcano,

'and with all this magic about it's certainly worth trying.'

He drew such a lifelike picture of three sardines on the board that Bobby Brewster's mouth started to water and he almost wished it was teatime.

'Now all keep as quiet as mice and watch,' whispered Mr Limcano.

The boys had never before been known to keep so still. You could have heard a pin drop. It was a strain, but luckily they didn't have long to wait. Suddenly, like a streak of lightning, a funny-looking animal darted through the window, jumped on the blackboard, and started eating the sardines. And it was a picture squitten – just like the picture that Mr Limcano had drawn, but had disappeared. Indeed, it *was* Mr Limcano's picture of Peeper the squitten. And, without knowing it, he *had* drawn a magic picture.

Silently Mr Limcano crept up to the board with a duster in his hand. Then he suddenly pounced and rubbed the blackboard clean, squitten, sardines, descriptions and all.

'Got you!' he cried – and that was that.

But what an exciting episode it had been, hadn't it? And all because Bobby Brewster is lucky enough to go to a school where there is a magic schoolmaster.

Don't you wish you did?

Desk diary

It is nice to receive presents at any time, but when they come quite unexpectedly on a day which isn't Christmas or your birthday, it is even more exciting. And that is exactly what happened to Bobby Brewster one evening in the middle of December the year before last.

His father came home from the office and said, 'Bobby I've got something useful for you.'

'What is it?' asked Bobby.

'Aha!' said Mr Brewster mysteriously.

'*Please* tell me,' cried Bobby.

'Aha!' repeated Mr Brewster.

'Don't tease the child. Tell him what it is,' said Mrs Brewster.

'Well,' said Mr Brewster, 'I have been given two of these, so I thought Bobby might like one of them.' And he took a book out of his brief-case and handed it to Bobby. It had a smart blue cover with gold printing on it, which Bobby read slowly.

'Desk Dairy,' he said. 'Who gave it to you? The milkman?'

'You silly boy, it doesn't say Desk Dairy, it says Desk Diary,' said Mr Brewster.

'What's a desk diary?' asked Bobby Brewster.

'It's a book for writing in all your engagements,' explained Mr Brewster. 'There is a page for each day of the year, and if someone is coming to see you, or you are going to a party, you put it down on the page of the day it is going to happen. Then you keep it on your desk to remind you.'

'But I haven't got a desk,' said Bobby.

'Then keep it on the table in your bedroom,' said Mr Brewster. 'I'm sure it won't mind.'

'Oh, *thank* you, Father,' said Bobby. 'It's a lovely present.'

'I'm glad you like it,' said Mr Brewster. 'And be careful to enter your name and address and all your engagements very neatly.'

'Of course I will,' said Bobby, and he ran upstairs with his new desk diary.

On the front page it had a special space for putting NAME and ADDRESS, so the first thing that Bobby did was to write them down very carefully. Then a very funny thing happened.

Bobby turned to the next page, which was headed NOTES, and underneath, printed in red capitals, were the following words:

I'M A MAGIC DESK DIARY,
BUT DON'T TELL ANYONE
OR THE MAGIC WON'T WORK

Bobby could hardly believe his eyes. 'However can a desk diary be magic?' he thought.

He soon found out. He turned to the page for February 23rd, and on it was printed, in red capital letters:

BOBBY BREWSTER'S BIRTHDAY

which was perfectly true.

Then he turned back to his mother's birthday – January 2nd.

MRS BREWSTER'S BIRTHDAY

it said in red capitals.

BOBBY GIVES HER ONE SLIPPER AND A PACKET OF PINS

'That settles it,' thought Bobby. 'It *must* be magic if it says that, because what it says is perfectly true and I thought no one but me knew about it.'

Before I go on with the story, perhaps I'd better explain about the ONE SLIPPER AND A PACKET OF PINS. You see, although he knew his mother needed some new slippers, Bobby couldn't afford to buy a pair just for Christmas, and so he decided to give her one slipper for Christmas and one for her birthday. But it would be silly if she had to hop about on one leg for a week, wouldn't it? So he was going to give her the pair of slippers on Christmas Day, and explain that it was really two presents – and save the packet of pins just to give her something new on her birthday.

Well, by this time, Bobby was busy looking right through his desk diary, and he found it had *all* his family's birthdays entered in red capitals. Aunts, uncles, and cousins as well. And that wasn't all. Some of his school friends, whose birthdays he didn't even know, were in it too. On March 13th, for instance, it said:

BILLY SINGLETON'S BIRTHDAY

And when Bobby asked Billy Singleton when his birthday was, he found that the desk diary was quite right. As a matter of fact Billy Singleton was rather curious to know why Bobby had asked, but Bobby couldn't explain that his desk diary had told him without saying anything about the magic. So he just said 'Oh, I just want to know, that's all,' which made Billy Singleton more curious than ever.

But it was when the new year began that Bobby found out just how magic his desk diary really was. It didn't just tell birthdays. Oh dear me, no.

It started showing in red capitals the things that were going to happen. And not always nice things, either. One Saturday in January Miss Trenham's school had a football match, and when Bobby looked in his diary that morning it said in red:

MISS TRENHAM'S SCHOOL – 2
ST JOSEPH'S SCHOOL – 3
BOBBY BREWSTER KICKS THE BALL
INTO HIS OWN GOAL

When that game took place Bobby played badly because he was very anxious not to kick the ball the wrong way, but at last he became so fed up with himself that he *did* take a big kick, and sure enough the ball *did* go into his own goal, much to the disgust of the rest of the team.

After a time Bobby found himself trying to catch the desk diary out. When it said he was going to do one thing he tried to do something else, but it never worked. One day during the summer term, for instance, the diary said:

CRICKET
BOBBY BREWSTER MAKES 15

which was a jolly good score for him. Well, in the game that afternoon Bobby *tried* to get out, but he couldn't. When he hit catches in the air the boys dropped them all. By the time he had actually made fifteen runs he was so confident that he was sure he could score another run and prove the diary wrong. He never had the chance. It started to pour with rain and the game was stopped. And to make matters worse, when he got home and looked in his desk diary, two words had been added, and it said:

CRICKET
BOBBY BREWSTER MAKES 15 NOT OUT

So it was right twice over!

But the most extraordinary thing happened in

October. One morning during that month Bobby looked in his desk diary and it said:

BOBBY BREWSTER BREAKS A LEG

Well – what would you have done? First of all Bobby pretended that he wasn't well and tried to stay in bed, but his mother wasn't having any of that. After she had taken his temperature and made sure it was normal, she told him not to be silly and packed him off to school. He was extra careful going along the road, and wouldn't play with the other boys when he got to school, which surprised them because he is usually in the middle of any fighting that goes on in the playground. All that day he kept very quiet and then he went home. At the tea table, as usual, he started to tilt his chair back without realizing he was doing it. Do *you* ever tilt your chair back when you are sitting down? Bobby Brewster often does. His mother keeps on saying, 'Bobby, *don't* tilt your chair back. It's dangerous.' But it doesn't make any difference. The next time he sits at table he starts tilting his chair again.

But that day he tilted it once too often. The

legs of the chair suddenly slipped, and Bobby Brewster was thrown backwards with a great big crash.

'Oh! *Oh!*' he cried, and started hopping about on one leg.

'Whatever's the matter?' asked his mother.

'I've broken my leg,' cried Bobby.

'Don't be ridiculous,' said his mother. 'If you had really broken a leg you would never have been able to get up. Don't make such a fuss. It serves you right anyway, for tilting your chair.'

Then she picked up the fallen chair.

'You careless boy,' she said. 'It's not your own leg you've broken. It's the chair leg.'

And he had – one of the legs of his chair had snapped right across.

He was very quiet for the rest of tea, and then he went up to his bedroom and looked in his desk diary. You'll never guess what was printed in it – in red capitals, of course.

AHA! THAT CAUGHT YOU. YOU THOUGHT YOU WERE GOING TO BREAK YOUR *OWN* LEG, DIDN'T YOU? I NEVER SAID SO. I

JUST SAID 'BOBBY BREWSTER BREAKS A LEG.' AND YOU HAVE, YOU SILLY BOY

Well, no one likes being called a 'silly boy', do they? Especially by their own desk diary. So although it was only October and there were several weeks to go before the year was used up, Bobby closed his desk diary and didn't look at it again until January 1st the next year. And by that time it was out of date anyway, so he threw it away in the waste paper basket.

I don't blame him, do you? After all, who *wants* to know what is going to happen all the time? When you do, it's not nearly so exciting when it *does* happen, is it?

When Mr Brewster brought home another desk diary for Bobby that December, he took it upstairs and looked inside rather anxiously on the page headed NOTES.

And for once he was jolly pleased to find that it *wasn't* magic.

Scrumpistick

Don't you think that some of the advertisements on television are silly? Bobby Brewster does. And what stupid voices some of the people use! Those sm-o-o-o-th s-i-l-k-y voices that ooze out while girls with a dreamy expression in their eyes are stroking their hair. Or the men who shout: 'Go out and buy one NOW.' As if you could. Half the time they're shouting it at about ten o'clock at night, when all the shops are shut and you couldn't go out and buy one, even if you wanted to.

The fact remains, however silly the advertisements may sound, people often do go out and buy the things the next day. And that is exactly what happened to Bobby Brewster one day last summer, with the most extraordinary results.

It was a rainy Friday afternoon during the holidays. The Brewsters had planned to go on a picnic the next day, and Bobby felt so worried about the rain that he turned on the television to cheer himself up. Then came the advertisements. There were the usual washing powders and dog foods at first, and then a man appeared on the screen.

'I'm going to let you into a secret,' he said. 'But it won't stay a secret for long, because soon everybody will know about it. If you are going on a picnic, you simply *must* take Scrumpistick to eat. It's delicious.'

Then his family ran in and started dancing round and round a picnic basket, singing a song to the tune of 'Here we go round the mulberry bush'.

After that they stood in a line, each holding up a bar of Scrumpistick, and they all said together:

'Scrumpistick. It's delicious! M-m-m-m,' – and made a delicious sort of face.

Then they faded out. And about time, too.

Well, Bobby thought it was rather a silly advertisement at the time, but when the next morning was fine and his mother asked, 'What shall we take to eat on our picnic?' the first thing that Bobby thought of was Scrumpistick, so the advertisement can't have been as silly as all that. And sure enough Mrs Brewster packed the picnic basket complete with three bars of Scrumpistick and off they went.

Do you *always* enjoy picnics? I'm afraid I don't. There *are* times, of course, when everything goes right. The weather is perfect, there are not many people about, and there are *no* wasps. But I'm sorry to say that this was not one of those days.

In the first place they took far too long to find the spot to have their picnic at all. Mr Brewster kept on driving along and someone would say, 'There's a marvellous place,' but by that time they would have driven past it. Then Mr Brewster would see another opening ahead and slow down, only to find cars already parked there with lots of people sitting on the ground eating *their* picnics. And who wants to picnic in a crowd? This seemed to go on for ages, and by the time they did stop, I regret to say that they were not in the best of tempers.

Then things went from bad to worse. Mrs Brewster tipped over the thermos flask and spilt all the tea, Mr Brewster bit into an apple with a grub in it, and Bobby Brewster kicked a little mound that turned out to be an ants' nest. So in next to no time the sardine sandwiches were covered with ants.

But that wasn't all. There was a sudden thunderstorm, and it started to pour with rain. They were all caught without their raincoats, and had to gather up everything in a hurry and rush wet through into the car, leaving a pile of soggy sardine sandwiches for the ants to eat. And all they had left to eat themselves was three bars of Scrumpistick.

Mr Brewster bit into his bar of Scrumpistick. Then he made a face.

'What beastly stuff,' he said, 'I can't eat mine.'

'Nor can I,' said Mrs Brewster. 'It's all sticky

and sickly. Why on earth did you ask me to buy this stuff, Bobby?'

'Because the man on the television said it was delicious for a picnic,' said Bobby.

'Well, someone ought to tell him that he wants his head examined,' said Mr Brewster.

Secretly Bobby agreed with him, but he wasn't going to show it, and anyway he was hungry. So he ate his bar of Scrumpistick far too quickly and pretended to enjoy it.

But not for long. Mr Brewster was so anxious to get home that he drove rather fast, and Bobby began to feel ill. And the moment they reached home he rushed indoors and upstairs and was very sick.

And that was the end of a not-so-perfect picnic.

Poor Bobby went to lie on his bed for most of the afternoon, and by teatime he felt better. It was still raining and everybody was rather miserable, so after tea when Bobby was by himself in the sitting-room he turned on the television to cheer himself up. And who do you think appeared on the screen? That silly man again. What made it worse was that he was saying:

'If you are going on a picnic, you simply must take Scrumpistick to eat. It's delicious.'

Without thinking Bobby Brewster shouted back, 'That's nonsense. We *went* on a picnic, and we *took* some Scrumpistick to eat. Mother and Father couldn't finish theirs, and I ate a whole bar and it made me sick. It's beastly stuff.'

By this time the screen had gone blank and a notice come on to say, 'Normal service will be resumed shortly,' and Bobby thought to himself, 'Wouldn't it be wonderful if that silly man had really heard me!'

Then a very funny thing happened. After a few moments the television started again and the silly man reappeared on the screen.

'I'm going to let you into a secret,' he said, 'but it won't be a secret for long because soon everyone will know about it. If you are going on a picnic, whatever you do *don't* take Scrumpistick to eat. It's beastly stuff.'

Bobby Brewster could hardly believe his ears, but he must have heard right because the family came and danced round the picnic basket singing:

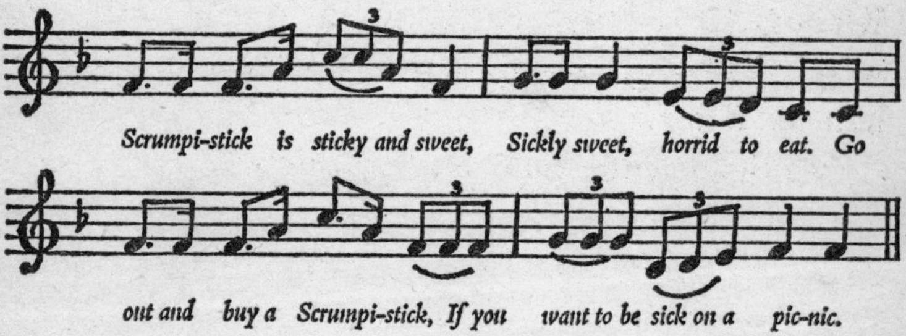

Then they stood in a line, each holding up a bar of Scrumpistick, and all said together:

'Scrumpistick. It's *beastly* stuff! Eeeough' – and made a sick sort of face.

Well, by this time Bobby Brewster thought that the Scrumpistick he had eaten must have made him not only sick but silly in the head. But he soon changed his mind. For a short time he sat looking in a dazed way at the other advertisements, and then there was a ring at the front door and he went to answer it. His friend Willie Watson was at the door, looking very excited.

'I've just seen the *funniest* advertisement for Scrumpistick on the television,' he said. 'It was *marvellous*. They all made fun of it and finished up by saying, "Scrumpistick. It's beastly stuff. Eeeough!" It made me laugh so much that I simply had to go straight out and buy some. And here's a bar for you.'

'No thank you,' said Bobby Brewster.

School tie

Miss Trenham's school colours are green and gold. Very smart they look too, when the school flag is proudly flying below the Union Jack on important days. The school motto is 'Fight for the right', which is all very well, but apt to cause unnecessary battles. The trouble is that different boys have different ideas as to what *is* the right.

When Bobby Brewster first wore his green and gold school tie, he was very proud and took great care of it. He even went to the trouble of putting it under the mattress of his bed every night and sleeping on it, so that the creases were squashed out. Unfortunately all this care didn't last, and Bobby soon began to take his smart school tie for granted.

The first lapse came when he spilled soup all over it through being in too much of a hurry to eat his dinner. Then he left his tie lying on the lawn one afternoon and the cat got hold of it. Naturally this didn't improve it, and it began to look more like a piece of coloured chewed string than a school tie.

But that wasn't all. There had been some excuse for being just careless with his tie, although it was a pity. But Bobby started using it for things that ties should never be made to do.

For instance, one warm night he wanted to keep his window open wide and the sash-cord had broken. There was no string in the bedroom and he couldn't be bothered to go downstairs and find some, so he used his tie to fix the window. What with the tight knotting and the damp dew, it was just as well that the next morning was Saturday and he was wearing an open collar. The tie still looked rather bedraggled on Sunday, though, and hardly fit to wear to church.

One day the following week the boys decided to have a tug-of-war competition during play break. They didn't ask Miss Trenham for a piece of rope, because they thought she might object to the idea altogether, so what do you think they used?

Bobby Brewster's school tie.

On the same afternoon, Bobby was going home from school when he saw Frisky Henderson, the neighbour's dog, barking and making a general nuisance of himself in somebody else's garden.

Now Frisky Henderson being a nuisance is nothing unusual, but Bobby Brewster is fond of the dog in spite of everything, and he thought he had better take him home before he got into trouble. That was easier said than done without a lead, so what do you think Bobby tied to Frisky's collar?

His school tie.

This time rather a peculiar thing happened. When Frisky was safely home, Bobby couldn't undo the tie from the collar. He has quite strong fingers and can usually unravel any tight knot after fiddling with it. But not this time. In the end he had to ask Mr Henderson to help. After undoing it with a great deal of trouble, Mr Henderson thanked Bobby for bringing Frisky home, but suggested that in future it might be wiser not to use his school tie for a dog's lead.

The following week Bobby had forgotten all about this advice and used his school tie for something even worse. Once again the boys wanted some fun at playtime, and on this occasion they chose a three-legged race. Bobby Brewster was most enthusiastic about the idea and paired up with Willie Watson. Of course, you can guess what happened, can't you?

They tied their legs together with Bobby Brewster's school tie.

Well – they won the race all right, but soon lost their enthusiasm, because after that an awkward thing happened. They couldn't untie their legs. They couldn't, really. There they were, tied together in the middle of the playground, with lessons just starting. All they could do was to hop into class still tied together and hope for the best.

Mr Limcano was taking the lesson – and it was a jolly good thing he was, because Miss Trenham might have been far more annoyed than he was when he saw them hop into class tied together. He first made a typical schoolmaster's joke.

'I knew Bobby Brewster and Willie Watson were close friends,' he said, 'but I didn't know they were inseparable.'

Actually he was nearer the truth than he imagined, because, do you know, even Mr Limcano couldn't untie the knot in the tie. He tried every way, by fiddling, and then by pushing a screwdriver in between the tight folds and easing it open, but nothing would work. In the end Mr Limcano said, 'Well, Bobby, you can't spend the rest of your life tied to Willie Watson. It would be most inconvenient for both of you.

I'm afraid you may get into trouble with your mother and father, but it's your own fault for using your school tie for an improper purpose. We shall have to cut you apart.'

Then the funniest thing of the whole story happened. Mr Limcano felt in his pocket for a penknife and knelt down to cut the school tie in two. But it wasn't necessary. The tie had already fallen apart without anyone touching it. It had, really. Anyone would have thought it had heard what Mr Limcano said.

Well, all this was most extraordinary and might have resulted in considerable discussion. But so much teaching time had been lost that Mr Limcano insisted on going straight ahead with the history lesson, and no more was said.

Except by Bobby Brewster, that is. When he undid his tie while undressing that evening he said to himself, 'This wretched school tie might have got me into serious trouble today.'

At least he thought he said it to himself, but he can't have done, because a voice replied, 'I'm not a wretched school tie.'

'I beg your pardon?' asked Bobby Brewster.

'I said I'm not a wretched school tie,' repeated the tie. 'It's you who are a wretched schoolboy.'

'Why do you think so?' asked Bobby.

'Because you ill-treat your smart school tie, of which you ought to be very proud,' explained the school-tie.

'I *am* proud of it,' protested Bobby.

'You *were* proud of it when you first had it, you mean,' persisted the school tie. 'But it doesn't show much sign of pride when you use it for a window sash-cord, a tug-of-war rope, a dog's lead and, worst of all, a three-legged race leg-tier, does it?'

'I suppose that's true enough,' agreed Bobby Brewster.

'I tried to warn you before that you were behaving unfairly towards me,' said the tie. 'Don't you remember how difficult Mr Henderson found it to untie me from Frisky's collar, and told you afterwards not to use your tie for things like that?'

'Now you mention it, I do,' said Bobby.

'Well, a fat lot of notice you took, didn't you?' said the tie.

'I'm very sorry,' said Bobby apologetically. 'I suppose I have been rather silly. You're a very clever tie to be able to point out my mistakes to me, and I promise that in future I'll take great care of you.'

'Thank you,' said the tie. 'I only hope you're not too late. I'm covered in gravy and I'm a funny, pulled-out shape, but we shall have to hope that no one notices it and throws me away.'

'Just you leave it to me,' said Bobby. 'I promise you that won't happen.'

Bobby more than kept his promise. First of all, to his mother's great astonishment, he took his school tie to the dry cleaner's and insisted on paying from his pocket-money to have it cleaned and pressed. And from that day to this, not only has he taken great care to tie it into a neat knot whenever he puts it on in the morning, but he has slept with it under his mattress every night to keep it well pressed.

Isn't that sensible of him?